THE 5TH QUARTER

A Parent's Guide to Preparing Student-Athletes
for Life Beyond the Game

MARTY MCNAIR

Copyright © 2025 by Marty McNair

International copyright laws protect this book. All rights reserved. Except for reviews, No part of this book may be reproduced, distributed, or transmitted in any form or by any means, including photocopying, recording, or other electronic or mechanical methods without the prior written permission of the publisher, except in the case of brief quotations embodied in critical reviews and certain other noncommercial uses permitted by copyright law.

International Standard Book Number 978-1-7348-1776-8 Paperback

While the author has made every effort to provide accurate internet addresses at the time of publication, neither the publisher nor the author assumes any responsibility for errors or changes after publication. Further, the publisher has no control over and does not assume any responsibility for the author or third-party websites or their content. Some names, businesses, places, events, locales, incidents, and identifying details inside this book have been changed to protect the privacy of individuals.

Published and Printed in the United States of America by Marty McNair.

Cover and interior design: iamkerrywatson.com

Email: contact@thejordanmcnairfoundation.org

Website: thejordanmcnairfoundation.org

Social Media:
IG thejordanmcnairfoundation,
Linkedin @Martin Marty McNair

DEDICATION

I dedicate this book to my son, Jordan Martin McNair, whose legacy I have committed to carrying on through the mission of the Jordan McNair Foundation.

I always believed Jordan had the potential to play on Sundays. I never imagined that his story would go on to save the lives of so many.

This book is for him and for every parent, student-athlete, and family striving to prepare for the journey ahead—both on and off the field.

CONTENTS

INTRODUCTION

Why This Book Exists

This book wasn't born out of theory or research, it was born out of experience—hard, painful, personal experience.

In June 2018, my son **Jordan McNair** passed away at the age of nineteen from a 100 percent preventable heat-related injury during an off-season football conditioning workout at the **University of Maryland**. It was the first day of summer workouts, and like most parents, we assumed he was in good hands. We trusted the process, the coaching staff, and the environment that was supposed to nurture him as both an athlete and a young man. But what we didn't know was that there were cracks in the system, cracks that would eventually lead to Jordan's death.

Jordan wasn't just a football player. He was a **leader, a big brother, a loyal friend**, and a kid with an infectious smile. He had dreams of playing at the highest level, and even more than that, he dreamed of building a life beyond football. He was kind, coachable, and dedicated, but he was also just like any other teenager learning, growing, and figuring out who he was.

On May 29, 2018, during a routine conditioning workout, Jordan suffered from **exertional heatstroke**, a condition that, with proper and timely intervention, is 100 percent survivable. But that day, something went terribly wrong. Proper emergency procedures weren't followed, and the opportunity to save his life was missed. He spent the next two weeks fighting for his life in the hospital, but on **June 13, 2018**, Jordan passed away.

In that moment, my life and the life of my family changed forever. We were left with grief, anger, and countless unanswered questions. But after those initial waves of emotion passed, one thing became clear: **we had to turn our pain into purpose.**

That purpose became the **Jordan McNair Foundation**, which is dedicated to promoting awareness and education about heat-related injuries, as well as advocating for student-athlete safety. Since Jordan's passing, we've made it our mission to ensure that no other family has to endure the same tragedy.

Why This Book Is Different

After starting the foundation, I wrote my first book, *Can My Child Play? The Questions We Should Have Asked*, which was focused on educating parents about the **right questions to ask** when it comes to your child playing for any sports organization as well as the recruitment process. That book encouraged parents to be more aware, more engaged, and more prepared when sending their children off to play sports at the youth, high school, and collegiate level.

This book, however, takes things a step further. While *Can My Child Play?* was about **asking the right questions**, *The 5th Quarter* is about **taking action**. It's a **shorter, more focused guide**, specifically designed to **prepare both parents and student-athletes** for the realities of college life, not just on the field, but off it as well.

The goal of this book is simple: to help parents and student-athletes build the skills they'll need to thrive in a collegiate environment, whether that's learning how to advocate for themselves, protect their physical and mental well-being, or manage new financial responsibilities. It's about preparing them for **life after sports**.

Why This Book Matters

The reality is, being a student-athlete at the collegiate level is tough. There are high expectations, constant pressures, and countless decisions that young athletes have to make every day. It's not just about sports; it's about balancing academics, social life, and for many, newfound financial opportunities through **name, image, and likeness (NIL)** deals.

As parents, we want to be there for every tough moment, every hard decision, every difficult choice. But the truth is, we can't. By the time they get to college, our voice gets smaller.

That's why it's so important to teach them how to think critically, act responsibly, and advocate for themselves when it matters most.

This book will walk you through the lessons I wish I had taught Jordan earlier—lessons about **leadership, self-advocacy, financial literacy**, and **mental health**. It will help you prepare your child for life after sports, because one day, the game will end, but life will keep going. And when it does, they'll need more than athletic skills. They'll need life skills.

Final Note

Jordan's story is one of loss, but it's also one of **legacy**. His passing sparked a movement toward better safety standards in high school and collegiate athletics, and it inspired this book. My hope is that by sharing what I've learned through personal experience, hindsight, and painful lessons, I can help you better prepare your child for the road ahead.

No parent should ever have to bury their child. No family should ever have to endure what we did. While we can't control everything that happens, we can do our part to prepare our student-athletes not just for their time on the field, but for life after the final whistle blows.

Let's get started.

CHAPTER 1

THE RECRUITMENT PITCH

When Jordan started getting recruited, the process felt surreal. It was exciting for him, but as parents, it was also nerve-racking. College coaches were visiting his high school, sending letters, and making promises that sounded larger than life. At one point, Jordan had so many letters that he filled up multiple shoeboxes with them. He was being recruited by almost every major school in the country—it was a proud moment for our family, but it was also overwhelming.

We visited several schools together, including **Ohio State**, where **Coach Urban Meyer** gave me a piece of advice that I still carry with me today. He said:

> *"Mr. McNair, whether you choose Ohio State or not, make sure you get a lifetime scholarship. These schools will get everything they can out of your athlete—you do the same."*

That advice hit home. Schools want what your child can offer **on the field**, but you have to make sure your child gets what they need **off the field** too—because at the end of the day, **the ball will stop bouncing, and the game will end**.

Jordan ended up choosing the **University of Maryland (UMD)**, after being heavily recruited by them. He was hooked by their promises of building a dynasty, winning championships, and playing close to home. During one of their early conversations, a UMD coach asked him:
"If the new Air Jordans dropped this weekend, would you drive to Philly or Baltimore to get them?"

Of course, Jordan said, "Baltimore." That question played on his connection to home, and it worked. He was locked in. He begged me to let him commit, and after much thought, we decided as a family that UMD was the right fit.

But here's a lesson I wish I knew back then:
Recruitment is a pitch—a well-rehearsed, emotional pitch designed to hook your child.

I'm sure that question about the Air Jordans probably hooked most of the recruits that year. In fact, that season turned out to be one of Maryland's best recruiting classes ever. The coaches knew exactly how to mentally engage seventeen- and eighteen-year-old recruits. They knew that things like **new sneakers, team gear, sweatsuits, and unlimited access to exclusive apparel** would excite them—and it worked.

And it's not just the student-athletes who get caught up in the pitch. As parents, we do too. Imagine visiting a school with a **successful winning track record**. I almost got caught up in the blinding light of the **championship rings sparkling in the showcase** at the Ohio State football building, surrounded by **NFL helmets of current and former players**. It's easy to be impressed by what's on display—because that's exactly what they want you to focus on.

However, the recruiting landscape has **changed significantly** since Jordan was being recruited. That **"lifetime scholarship"** Coach Meyer educated me on was significant back then and still is today. But student-athletes today are **different**—they know their **value**. The reality of **pay-to-play NIL deals** and the **transfer portal** has complicated a once simpler process. Decisions that were once based primarily on scholarships and playing time now involve much more: **contracts, branding, endorsements, and the realistic possibility of transferring to another school if things don't go as planned**.

I emphasize this: **do not let your child navigate these life decisions by themselves**. The more educated you are, the safer and better informed everyone will be when facing these decisions. Recruitment is no longer just about picking a school —it's about choosing the right environment that will set your child up for success, both during their athletic career and long after it ends.

The Reality Behind the Dream

As parents of student-athletes who receive significant interest from colleges, it's natural to believe there's a real chance that they'll play on the **big stage**—or maybe even on **Sundays** one day. When recruiters come knocking, it's easy to feel like your child is destined for greatness, and there's nothing wrong with believing in their potential.

But the reality is far different, and the statistics tell a humbling story:

- Only **6 percent of high school student-athletes** go on to play at the NCAA level.

- Of those, just **1.6 percent of college football players** make it to the NFL.

- The odds of reaching the NBA are only **2-3 percent** for college basketball players.

Like many parents reading this book, I believed our son, **Jordan McNair**, had the potential to play at the next level. He was talented, driven, and hardworking, and we were confident that he had what it took to succeed on the field. But as the recruitment process unfolded, I began to realize that while **athletic talent gets you noticed**, it's **preparation, asking the right questions, and prioritizing safety** that truly set your child up for long-term success—in sports and in life.

Core Message

Recruitment is about more than just playing time, championships, and scholarships. It's about finding a program that will:

- **Protect your child** on and off the field,

- **Prepare them for life after sports**, and

- **Support them physically, mentally, and emotionally** during their time at school.

So don't get blinded by the bling of championship rings and promises of professional careers. Those things are great, but they don't tell the full story. Your main goal as a parent is to **protect your child's future**, both on and off the field.

> **"Don't get blinded by the bling of championship rings. Focus on the 5th Quarter —life beyond sports."**

Takeaways for Parents

1. **Recruitment is a well-rehearsed pitch, not a promise.** Recruiters are trained to sell you and your child on their school and program. It's their job. Your job is to look beyond the pitch and **ask the hard questions** about things that truly matter.

2. **Stay grounded and don't get caught up in the excitement.** It's easy to get swept up by promises of championships, NFL dreams, and the glitz of high-level programs. But your focus should be on whether the school offers a safe and supportive environment for your child.

3. **Ask about more than playing time.** While recruiters are sitting in your living room—or, in our case, at the kitchen table eating a spaghetti dinner— they'll tell you everything you want to hear. That's why asking the hard questions is extremely important. Don't be like me and countless other parents who only asked one question:
"Can Jordan get some playing time?"
As parents, we often hesitate to ask tough questions because we fear it might hurt our child's opportunity. But remember, your goal isn't to please the recruiter— your goal is to **protect your child's future**. Ask about safety protocols, mental health resources, academic support, and what happens if your child gets hurt.

4. **Think beyond the game.** Recruitment is about finding a school that will prepare your child for life after sports. What kind of career support and alumni networks do they offer? How will they help your child transition into the next chapter of their life when the game ends?

5. **Stay involved and be informed.** Don't leave your child to navigate these decisions alone. The recruiting process is more complex today, with NIL deals, the transfer portal, and financial opportunities in play. The more informed you are, the better prepared you'll be to guide your child in making the right choice.

Conversation Starters with Your Student-Athlete

1. **"What excites you the most about this school, beyond just sports?"**
Help your child think beyond athletics and consider academics, campus life, and long-term opportunities.

2. **"What do you think life will be like after football (or basketball)?"**
This question helps your child start thinking about life after sports—something many student-athletes don't consider early enough.

3. **"If you felt unsafe or uncomfortable, who would you talk to?"**
Encourage your child to think about who they could turn to for help in difficult situations. Reinforce the importance of **self-advocacy**.

4. **"What questions do you want to ask the coaches during your visit?"**

Help your child take an active role in the recruitment process by preparing thoughtful questions that go beyond playing time.

Final Thoughts

Recruitment is an exciting and memorable experience, and it's something to be proud of. But it's also just the beginning. The promises made during recruitment are just that—promises. The real work begins once your child steps on campus.

By staying grounded, asking the right questions, and focusing on life beyond sports, you'll give your child the best chance to succeed—not just as an athlete, but as a well-rounded individual prepared for whatever life brings.

CHAPTER 2

THE OFFICIAL VISIT

When we decided as a family that Jordan would attend the **University of Maryland**, he was locked in. He was hooked by the idea of building a championship dynasty at UMD, and honestly, he was sold from the moment someone asked him about the **Air Jordans** he'd be receiving. He begged me to let him commit, but I wasn't ready to sign off just yet. I wanted to visit a few more schools that had shown interest in him before we made a final decision.

There's one recruiting visit in particular that stands out in my memory—when we met **Coach Urban Meyer** at Ohio State. During that visit, Coach Meyer gave me a piece of advice I'll never forget. He said, **"Mr. McNair, whether you decide to attend Ohio State or not, make sure you get a lifetime scholarship. These schools will get everything they can out of your athlete—you do the same."**

That stuck with me. Ultimately, we chose Maryland because of that promise of a **lifetime scholarship** and the long-term benefits of **life after sports**, including alumni networking when it came time for Jordan to transition into a career.

The Weekend of the Official Visit

The official visit is a big milestone in the recruitment process. It usually happens after your student-athlete has **committed to a school and signed their letter of intent**. It's the weekend when the red carpet gets rolled out, the coaching staff wines and dines the parents with lavish dinners, pays for lodging if you're coming from out of town, and makes sure you feel like royalty.

For your student-athlete, it's a chance to **meet their future teammates** and start building those relationships. But it's also a moment when you, as a parent, will get a glimpse of what your child is made of. Will they be a **leader**? A **follower**? Or someone who's easily influenced by their new peers?

I had my concerns, not because I didn't trust Jordan, but because I knew what college environments could be like. I'd seen it all before. At the time, I owned a **behavioral health program in Baltimore City**, and one of our go-to tools for accountability was a **ten-panel instant-read urinalysis cup**. It tested every substance from marijuana to opiates and everything in between. If we suspected a client was under the influence, we'd hand them a cup and ask for a sample, with a staff member posted outside the restroom door.

That's why, before we left for UMD that evening, I asked Jordan to stop by my house. He had no idea what I was about to do. When he arrived, I handed him an instant-read cup, and said, **"Fill it up."**

He looked at me like I'd lost my mind, but he went ahead and did it. When he returned, I gave him what I call my "scare tactic" speech.

"Son, you see these ten substances? This is your first weekend visit to college. I've always taught you to be a leader, not a follower. This weekend is your test to see what you're made of. When you get back on Sunday, I'm going to give you another test. If you come up positive for any of these substances, I need your car back, and you'll be catching the bus to school. I don't know how you'll get to your trainer, but you'll figure it out. The consequences will be tough."

I continued: **"Pay attention to the new recruits who are drinking out of red cups and smoking weed. Just observe the room and see who's following the crowd."**

Now, deep down, I knew Jordan wasn't the type of kid to get caught up in that. But he didn't know that I knew. I had to instill in him the **fear of making bad decisions**. It was all I had at the time. Looking back, I realize it was a bit extreme—but I didn't have a guide or a blueprint to follow.

That's why I wrote this book—so you don't have to resort to some outrageous scare tactics like I did. Instead, you'll have the tools to prepare your child in advance for moments like these.

Takeaways for Parents

1. **The official visit is about more than impressing parents.** While the school will go out of its way to make you feel special, the most important part of the visit is how your student-athlete handles themselves in this new environment. Pay attention to how they interact with future teammates and whether they show leadership qualities.

2. **Teach your student-athlete to observe, not just participate.** College environments, especially during official visits, can be full of temptations—drinking, partying, peer pressure, and risky behaviors. Encourage your child to observe what's happening around them before jumping in. Being aware of their surroundings is a key life skill.

3. **Use this weekend as a teaching moment.** The official visit is a great opportunity to talk about leadership, decision-making, and peer pressure. It's also a chance to reinforce your expectations and values before they enter college life.

Conversation Starters with Your Student-Athlete

1. **"What did you notice about your future teammates? Do you see yourself fitting in with them?"**

This question encourages your student-athlete to reflect on the people they'll be spending the next several years with.

2. **"Did you see any situations where people were following the crowd instead of leading? How did you feel about that?"**

This opens the door for a discussion about peer pressure and making independent decisions.

3. **"What do you think it means to be a leader on and off the field?"**

This helps reinforce the importance of leadership, not just in sports but in life.

4. **"If you ever feel uncomfortable in a situation, who can you go to for help?"**

This question helps prepare your child to seek support when they need it—whether it's from a coach, teammate, or trusted adult.

Final Thoughts

The official visit is a key moment in your student-athlete's journey. It's their first real taste of college life, and it's also a chance for you to see how they handle themselves in a new environment. Use it as an opportunity to talk openly about leadership, decision-making, and peer pressure.

You may not be able to prevent every bad decision, but by planting the seeds early and having honest conversations, you'll give them the tools to make better decisions when it matters most.

CHAPTER 3

ARE THEY REALLY READY?

Every parent wants to believe their child is ready for college. And on paper, maybe they are.

They're smart. They're talented. They have good grades, and they've got a highlight reel that could make any recruiter's jaw drop. That's the version of "ready" that most parents focus on.

But let me ask you a different question—one that doesn't get asked enough:

Is your child ready for life and the experiences ahead of them?

Not just the tests, the practices, or the games. I'm talking about the emotional, mental, and life challenges that come with being a college athlete. **Are they ready for that?**

If you're being honest with yourself, you know the answer. You know your child. You know their strengths, but you also know their weaknesses. You know if they're quick to ask for help or if they'll suffer in silence because they don't want to "look weak." You know if they're the type to stand up for themselves or if they'll go along with the crowd to fit in.

The truth is, college isn't just about academics and athletics. It's about their **independence**. It's about being on your own for the first time—waking yourself up for six a.m. workouts, feeding yourself when you're exhausted, and deciding how to handle situations you've never encountered before. No coach, no recruiter, and no teammate is going to do that for them.

A Funny Story About Readiness

A funny story that always reminds me of the value of a mother's love in the recruitment process comes from my good friend Al P. Al's a die-hard baseball fan now, but back in the 1960s and 1970s, he was a talented high school baseball player himself. He loves to tell the story of how, during his senior year, he was being recruited by a few out-of-state schools. He thought he was on the fast track to playing college ball. But his mother? Well, she had other ideas.

Al says, "One day, a recruiter was sitting right there in our living room, talking about scholarships and opportunities. My mom didn't miss a beat—she looked that recruiter dead in the eye and said, *'He'll be dead within a week if he leaves home!'*"

Al laughs every time he tells that story because, in hindsight, he admits she wasn't wrong. His mother knew him better than anyone. While he had the talent to play baseball, she also knew he wasn't ready for the world outside of their neighborhood. As much as she wanted to see him succeed, she wanted to protect him more.

As parents, we often see beyond the highlight reels and scholarship offers. We know if our kids are truly ready for the world—or if they still need time to grow.

Don't send your child to college unprepared.

A friend of mine once told me a story about sending her daughter to college in Florida on a basketball scholarship. One day, her daughter called home, hysterical. She was crying on the phone, upset, and frustrated. Her mom was concerned and asked, "What's wrong?"

Her daughter explained that the team had left her behind when they went to the grocery store.

Now, let me pause for a second. Think about that. They left her behind for a grocery store trip. No emergency. No crisis. But in that moment, it felt like one for her daughter.

So, what did her mom do? She didn't panic. She didn't call the coach. She didn't book a flight to Florida to "save" her daughter. Instead, she said something every parent needs to hear:

"What do you want me to do, come to Florida and take you to the grocery store?"

Her daughter paused.

Her mom continued, "Here's what you're going to do. You're going to calm down. Then you're going to grab your backpack, hop on your bike, and ride to the store yourself."

And that's exactly what her daughter did.

It might sound small, but this is what happens when your child isn't prepared to solve problems on their own. Something as simple as a missed grocery run can feel like the end of the world when you're eighteen, living alone for the first time, and faced with a problem you've never had to solve before.

The big lesson here? If your child isn't ready to solve simple problems like this, they definitely aren't ready for the bigger ones.

Are They Really Ready?

So, let me ask you again—and I want you to really think about this: **Is your child ready?**

- Are they ready to recognize peer pressure for what it is—and stand firm against it?

- Are they ready to advocate for themselves when something feels wrong with their body, even if a coach tells them to "push through it"?

- Are they ready to manage their money when they start earning from NIL deals?

- Are they ready to prioritize their mental health and recognize when they need help?

- Are they ready to solve basic problems without calling home for help?

If you're not 100 percent sure of your answers, that's okay. It doesn't mean your child isn't worthy of playing at the next level. It doesn't mean they're not talented enough, smart enough, or tough enough. **It just means there are things they still need to learn—and that's where you come in.**

As parents, we have a responsibility to fill in those gaps. It's not about doing everything for them, but it is about preparing them for what's coming.

That's what this book will do. It will help you ask better questions. It will help you prepare for the things you don't know.

This is your chance to get ahead of it. Your chance to make sure your child is ready for everything that's coming—not just the next practice or the next game, but the moments when no one's watching.

Key Themes Recap

- Independence isn't just about being away from home—it's about learning how to solve real-life problems.

- Emotional and mental readiness are just as important as athletic talent and academic preparation.

- Help your child develop self-advocacy skills so they can stand up for themselves when you're not there.

- Start conversations early about life skills like money management, mental health, and decision-making.

Reflection Questions for Parents

Take a moment to reflect on these questions:

1. When you think about your child being away from home, what worries you the most?

2. If your child faced a difficult decision—like standing up to a coach or reporting a safety issue—do you think they would have the courage to do it?

3. Have you ever had a conversation with your child about what it means to be legally "emancipated" at eighteen?

4. If your child experienced anxiety, stress, or depression at school, would they know where to go for help?

5. If your child missed a grocery trip, would they know how to figure it out—or would they call you, expecting you to solve it?

6. What life skills (cooking, budgeting, managing time) does your child still need to develop before leaving for college?

Conversation Starters for Parents and Student-Athletes

These are some of the most important conversations you can have with your child before they leave home. Use these questions to check in with them and see how prepared they feel:

1. "What's something you're excited about when you get to college? What's something that makes you nervous?"

2. "If a teammate or captain told you to 'push through' an injury, how would you handle it?"

3. "Do you know where you would go on campus if you needed to talk to someone about your mental health?"

4. "When you start earning NIL money, what's the first thing you want to do with it?"

5. "What's one life skill you think you still need to work on before you leave home?"

6. "If you missed a grocery trip and had no ride, how would you handle it?"

Now that you've thought about whether your child is really ready, it's time to focus on **the support system they'll need once they're in college**. No one succeeds in a vacuum. In the next chapter, we'll explore how to build a team around your student-athlete that will help them navigate the challenges of both sports and life.

CHAPTER 4

STAYING INVOLVED LEGALLY: HOW TO PROTECT YOUR CHILD'S FUTURE

By the time your child turns eighteen, the law considers them an adult. That means they're legally responsible for their own decisions—medical, financial, and educational. While it's a proud moment for any parent to see their child reach adulthood, it also comes with new challenges that most of us aren't prepared for.

Many parents don't realize that once their child is legally an adult, they lose access to critical information. Without the right legal protections in place, you might not be able to step in when it matters most—even in an emergency.

A Personal Story: The Question That Changed Everything

When our son Jordan was in the hospital fighting for his life due to severe complications from a heat-related injury,

Jordan's mother and I decided to seek legal representation. It was one of the hardest moments of our lives, and we knew we needed help navigating the situation.

At our very first meeting, the lawyer asked us a simple but life-changing question:
"Do you have a power of attorney for Jordan?"

We were confused. "No, why would we need one?" we asked.

His response hit us like a ton of bricks: **"Because at eighteen, he's emancipated—meaning he's legally an adult."**

Our immediate reaction was disbelief. "He still calls Tonya and asks if he can go out on Friday nights from college," we said.

But the lawyer's point was clear: legally, Jordan was now responsible for his own decisions, and without a power of attorney, we couldn't make critical decisions for him if he wasn't able to do so himself.

Right then and there, we saw the magnitude of not having those legal protections in place. I often think about the "what ifs" of our story.

- What if Jordan had been attending a school in another state, hundreds or even thousands of miles away from home?

- What if he had been on the West Coast or in the Midwest, where we couldn't get to him quickly?

These are the kinds of questions that haunt parents when the worst happens. Like most parents, we didn't have an "in the event of" mindset. We didn't think we'd ever be in a position where we'd need to make urgent medical, legal, or financial decisions for our child once he turned eighteen.

But the truth is, **no one thinks about this—until they have to.**

Falling in Love and Flunking Out: Another Parent's Story

Here's another story from a friend that illustrates why having legal protections in place is so important. Her son wasn't a student-athlete, but he was going away to college for the first time, just like so many other young adults. He attended a school in Tennessee, far from home, and everything seemed fine at first.

Long story short, he fell in love and completely lost sight of why he was at college in the first place: to get an education. He stopped focusing on his studies, and by the end of the second semester, he had flunked out. But here's the kicker: while home on break, he never told his mom that he had failed out of school. Instead, he went back, claiming everything was fine, and stayed with friends near campus.

His mom had no idea anything was wrong until a friend of hers who lived near the college happened to see her son off campus during class time and reached out to her. The college didn't inform her of his academic status. Why? Because they legally didn't have to. Her son was over eighteen years old and, therefore, legally emancipated.

Had she known about the legal steps she could have taken, she might have been able to intervene earlier. **This is why these legal protections matter:** they keep you aware and involved in your child's life, even after they turn eighteen.

NIL and Financial Protection: The Wild, Wild West

Now, let's talk about something even more complicated: money. With the rise of NIL deals, many college athletes are earning significant income for the first time in their lives. This is a game changer, and while we'll cover the NIL landscape in more detail later in the book, it's worth addressing here in the context of legal protections.

We, as parents, might still have moral, ethical, and emotional influence over our kids, but do we have legal influence? The answer is **no**, unless you have a power of attorney in place.

Think about it: would you be comfortable with your nineteen- or twenty-year-old suddenly having access to six-figure income deals and making major financial decisions on their own? Most of us wouldn't. It's not because we don't trust our kids, it's because we know they still have a lot to learn about managing money, contracts, and long-term financial planning.

Without the proper legal authority, you may not be able to help them when they need it most.

Action Steps: How to Protect Your Child Legally

If you're wondering how to protect your child legally once they turn eighteen, the answer is simple: **Set up a power of attorney (POA).**

A power of attorney gives you the legal authority to act on your child's behalf in certain situations, whether it's making medical decisions, accessing financial accounts, or handling educational matters. Here's a step-by-step guide to getting started:

1. **Consult with a lawyer:**
   Reach out to a family or estate planning attorney to discuss your options for setting up a power of attorney for your child. Some states may have specific requirements or forms, so it's important to get professional guidance.

2. **Set up two types of POAs:**

○ **Medical Power of Attorney:** This allows you to make medical decisions on your child's behalf if they're unable to do so.

○ **Financial Power of Attorney:** This gives you the ability to manage your child's financial matters, such as accessing bank accounts, signing contracts, and handling NIL deals, if applicable.

3. **Sign the necessary documents:**
Once everything is in place, make sure you and your child both sign the documents in the presence of a notary (if required by your state). Keep copies of the signed POAs in a safe place.

4. **Ensure access to medical, financial, and academic records:**
Work with your child to ensure that any required forms (such as HIPAA releases or FERPA waivers for educational records) are signed and submitted to their school and healthcare providers.

Key Themes Recap

- **By age eighteen, your child is legally an adult.** Without a power of attorney, you may not be able to step in when they need you most.

- **Medical and financial POAs ensure you can still help your child in critical situations.**

- **With the rise of NIL deals, financial protections are more important than ever.** Helping your child manage newfound income requires legal authority as well as guidance.

CHAPTER 5

IT'S OKAY TO ASK FOR HELP: SUPPORTING YOUR ATHLETE'S MENTAL WELL-BEING

The Early Signs: Jordan's ADHD Diagnosis

Jordan was diagnosed with attention deficit/ hyperactivity disorder (ADHD) at the end of his freshman year in high school. ADHD can make it difficult for people to concentrate, pay attention, organize, and focus. It can also interfere with daily life, such as social relationships and school or work performance. Before his diagnosis, one of Jordan's teachers had pointed out that something wasn't connecting when it came to his attention to detail. He struggled to retain information for long periods of time, which made school especially difficult.

I'll never forget the day he got caught using his phone to look up answers during a test—before we knew he had ADHD. At the time, I didn't understand what he was going through. I saw it as plain old cheating, and in frustration, I threatened to break his legs if he ever got caught cheating again. I didn't realize how overwhelmed he was, and when he broke down in tears, he admitted how hard it had become to keep up with the academic load as a new freshman in high school. Looking back, I can see that was a pivotal moment.

By his sophomore year, with the new ADHD diagnosis in hand, we worked with the school to set up an Individualized Education Plan (IEP) that documented the need for accommodations like extra time on tests and additional academic support. One thing that year stood out to me: I began taking him to school an hour early every day so he could work with a tutor or teacher in preparation for tests. His work ethic grew stronger, and he learned to push harder to retain information, despite the challenges.

As a family, we encouraged Jordan to **embrace his ADHD diagnosis** instead of feeling ashamed or negatively about it. We made it clear that it wasn't something to hide or be embarrassed by; it was simply something he had to learn to manage, just like any other challenge. This shift in mindset helped him approach academics more confidently, knowing that needing extra support didn't make him any less capable.

As Jordan's athletic success grew, so did college offers from programs across the nation. By his junior year, during a meeting with his pediatrician, we discussed the option of medication for managing his ADHD. Ultimately, we left the decision up to Jordan. He decided to give the medication a try, and the change was incredible—he went from being an average, above-passing student to a stellar student who scored exceptionally high on his SAT exam.

But as proud as we were of his progress, I often think about how overwhelming that experience must have been for him before he had a diagnosis, before he had support. Imagine being an undiagnosed ADHD freshman in high school, struggling to keep up. Now imagine being a collegiate freshman, away from home for the first time, facing all of those same academic pressures—plus the challenges of being a student-athlete—and having to navigate it all on your own.

The Mental Health Crisis in College Athletics

Jordan's story is just one example of how mental health can impact student-athletes, but he wasn't the only one dealing with challenges. Two of his college teammates, who also happened to be his roommates, faced serious struggles during their first year. One of them was admitted to a behavioral health unit early in the season, while the other mentally checked out after losing his position when a new coach came in. Instead of competing for his spot, he just gave up. He stayed on the team, but mentally, he was gone. Eventually, he entered the transfer portal.

At the time, in 2018, I don't know exactly what kind of mental health support was available to them. But what I do know is that today, mental health support is at the forefront of most collegiate athletic programs. Schools now recognize the toll that academic pressure, athletic performance, and social life can take on student-athletes. **Anxiety, depression, eating disorders, and substance abuse are four of the main mental health issues that plague college athletes.** These struggles are often made worse by the stress of academics, social pressures, and the challenge of adjusting to a new environment.

So, the question is: **How do we prepare our kids not only to recognize these struggles but to embrace, accept, and acknowledge the realities of their mental health?** The NCAA now mandates that mental health professionals be available at all of their member schools to support athletes when they need help. But here's the thing: **your child has to know when and how to seek that help.**

The Importance of Seeking Help

That's why it's critical to prepare your student-athlete to seek help when they need it most—especially when the resources are abundant. No matter how strong or independent they are, they need to know it's okay to ask for help, and that mental health is just as important as physical health.

Think about it: if your child sprains an ankle or pulls a hamstring, they'll run straight to the trainer. So why should it be any different when they're feeling anxious, overwhelmed, or depressed? If they're struggling mentally, they need to know it's okay to run to a counselor for help in the same way they'd run to a trainer for physical pain.

Key Lessons for Parents

- **Normalize mental health conversations at home.** Make it clear that mental health is just as important as physical health.

- **Teach your child how to recognize when something feels off.** Whether it's persistent anxiety, trouble sleeping, or feelings of isolation, they need to know the signs that it's time to reach out.

- **Help them understand the resources available.** Go over what support is offered by their college, whether it's counseling services, peer support groups, or online mental health resources.

- **Encourage self-advocacy.** Let your child know that asking for help is a sign of strength, not weakness.

Action Steps: How to Prepare Your Child

1. **Have regular check-ins before they leave for college.** Ask how they're feeling not just physically, but mentally and emotionally.

2. **Role-play scenarios.** Help your child practice what they might say if they're feeling overwhelmed and need to talk to a counselor or coach.

3. **Research the college's mental health services together.** Make sure your child knows where to go on campus if they need help.

4. **Model openness about mental health.** Share your own experiences with stress or anxiety. When they see you being open, they'll be more likely to open up themselves.

Final Thoughts on Mental Health

The pressures of college athletics are real. From academic stress to athletic performance to social life, it can all feel overwhelming. But by normalizing mental health conversations and teaching our kids how to seek help, we can set them up for success—not just on the field, but in life.

We, as parents, can't always prevent our children from experiencing mental health challenges, but we *can* equip them with the tools to manage those challenges, embrace their mental health diagnosis, and seek help when they need it most. With open communication, encouragement, and access to the right resources, they'll be better prepared to navigate the ups and downs of college life.

Preparing for External Pressures

As much as we can prepare our children to manage their internal struggles, we can't ignore the **external pressures** they'll face, especially when it comes to peer pressure and social influence.

For student-athletes, it's not just about handling the stress of balancing academics and sports. They'll also face moments when they're pressured to make quick decisions—moments that can have lasting consequences. Whether it's at a party, in a locker room, or even in a dorm room, the pressure to fit in or go along with the crowd can push them to make choices that could harm their future.

That's why, in the next chapter, we'll dive into **peer pressure and decision-making**—how to help your child recognize it, navigate it, and confidently say, "Nah, I'm good," when it matters most. You can't shield them from every difficult situation, but you *can* teach them how to think critically and make wise decisions in the moment.

CHAPTER 6

COOL FRIENDS, TOUGH CHOICES: NAVIGATING PEER PRESSURE IN COLLEGE

Peer pressure is going to be a constant reality for your student-athlete at the collegiate level as they search for their identity in life. Just think about how peer pressure felt for us growing up at their age. It was tough and challenging enough without social media—now imagine that added element for our kids today.

College life will be about making new friends, building relationships, joining fraternities or sororities, and just trying to find their way. As parents, we can't be there for every single experience, like a good angel and a bad angel on their shoulders, guiding them through every decision. That's why it's crucial to **plant the seeds of good decision-making early**, so they're equipped to handle those moments when they come. We can't stop peer pressure from happening, but at the very least, we can prepare them for what's ahead.

A Lesson from Warren Buffett

Over the years, I've shared a simple piece of advice with Jordan and countless student-athletes I've spoken to— something I once heard Warren Buffett say:
"Don't do anything that will be read negatively in the newspaper the next morning."

I added my own twist for Jordan:
"Don't do anything that will embarrass your parents the next day."

The message was always the same: think before you act. Don't make impulsive decisions in the moment that could come back to haunt you later.

The W.A.I.T. Method: What Am I Thinking?

One of the most important skills you can teach your student-athlete is how to **pause and think consequentially** before making a decision. I call it the **W.A.I.T. method**, which stands for
What Am I Thinking?

Encourage them to slow down and ask themselves that simple question before they respond to peer pressure or make a quick decision. Teach them that it's more than okay to **take a moment, play out the possible consequences in their**

head, and think about how their actions might affect them in the long run.

I always hoped that when Jordan or any of the athletes I worked with faced a difficult decision, they would hear those words in the back of their minds: **"Don't do anything that will embarrass my parents the next day."**

The reality is, maybe they will hear it—and maybe they won't, because in their minds, their friends are way cooler than us parents. But whether they hear it or not, the important thing is that we, as parents, plant those seeds early. Because even if they don't listen at first, those seeds will grow over time.

Jordan's Story: Seeing the Realities Firsthand

Jordan was no different when it came to peer pressure. He knew my stance on alcohol and drug experimentation. He did his senior project at my drug treatment facility for two weeks, where he saw firsthand the real-life consequences of poor decision-making and substance abuse. I even took him into a county jail, where he sat in on a group session with prisoners who struggled with alcohol and substance abuse. He had way more information than most of his teammates.

Still, peer pressure is a powerful force, and no amount of preparation can guarantee perfect decisions.

Imagine my surprise after he passed, when I finally cracked the code to his phone and saw videos of him at a college party with a beer in his hand. In one video, he was happily ranting about one of his teammates going to the NFL and how he'd be soon following in his footsteps. He was a "happy drunk," as the music blasted in the background and everyone around him laughed.

That's part of the college experience—it's inevitable. No matter how much we try to prepare our kids, they're going to make their own choices. Some of those choices might disappoint us, and some might make us laugh in hindsight. But the point isn't to shield them from every experience; the point is to teach them how to think before they act, so they have the tools to handle those moments responsibly.

Planting Seeds Early

College is a time when kids are figuring out who they are. They're meeting new people, forming new relationships, and facing social pressures on a daily basis. While we, as parents, can't be there for every decision they make, we *can* give them the tools to think critically and handle peer pressure when it comes their way.

It starts with conversations. It starts with planting those seeds early—the seeds of **good decision-making, self-awareness, and the ability to pause and reflect** before acting. We might not always see the results right away, but eventually, those seeds will grow.

In the next section, we'll dive deeper into how to role-play scenarios with your student-athlete, teach them how to recognize peer pressure in the moment, and help them practice responses like **"Nah, I'm good"**—empowering them to make decisions they won't regret later.

Role-Playing Scenarios and Action Steps: Preparing Your Athlete for Peer Pressure

It's one thing to tell your child to make smart decisions and think before they act, but it's another to **teach them how** to do that in real-life situations. The best way to prepare your student-athlete for peer pressure is to **practice real scenarios** with them. It may feel awkward at first, but walking through situations they might encounter in college can build their confidence and help them develop a natural response when faced with peer pressure.

Here are a few strategies and scenarios you can use:

1. Practice Saying "Nah, I'm Good"

One of the hardest things for any student-athlete or any young adult is saying no, especially when they feel pressure to fit in. Whether it's being offered alcohol at a party, being dared to do something risky, or being pressured to skip class, they need to feel comfortable saying no without hesitation.

A simple way to prepare them is to practice casual responses that allow them to bow out without feeling embarrassed. Keep it light, and remind them that they don't owe anyone an explanation. Sometimes a simple "Nah, I'm good" is all it takes.

Here's an example scenario to role-play:
Scenario: Your child is at a party, and someone hands them a drink. They don't want to drink because they have practice the next morning.

- **You:** "Okay, so you're at this party, and someone hands you a beer and says, 'Come on, just one drink, everyone's drinking.' What do you say?"

- **Your Child:** "I'd probably say no, but I don't know if I'd feel weird about it."

- **You:** "Try saying, 'Nah, I'm good. I've got practice tomorrow.' No need to overthink it. Just keep it short and move on. Most people won't push it if you sound confident."

The key is to **keep it simple, confident, and casual.** Practicing these responses helps your child feel less awkward when they're in a real situation.

2. Teach Them to W.A.I.T.

Peer pressure often happens in the heat of the moment, when there's little time to think. That's why teaching your student-athlete to **slow down and pause** before making a decision is so important. This is where the **W.A.I.T. Method** comes in.

Encourage your child to take a moment and ask themselves:

- **"What am I thinking?"**

- **"What are the potential consequences of this decision?"**

- **"Is this something I'll regret tomorrow?"**

Role-play a scenario where they feel pressured to do something impulsive, and walk them through the thought process:
Scenario: A group of teammates dares them to skip class and hang out instead.

- **You:** "Your teammates are all saying, 'Come on, just skip class—it's no big deal.' What's the first thing you do?"

- **Your Child:** "I'd probably pause and think about it."

- **You:** "Good. Now, play it out in your head. What happens if you skip class? How might that affect your grades or how your coach sees you?"

- **Your Child:** "I'd probably get in trouble, or maybe my coach would find out."

- **You:** "Exactly. Pausing to think it through gives you the chance to make a better decision. W.A.I.T.—What Am I Thinking?—is a way to slow down before you act."

3. Discuss the "24-Hour Rule"

Another helpful tool is the **24-Hour Rule**: if they're not sure about something, tell them to give it twenty-four hours before making a big decision. This works especially well for situations that involve peer pressure over time, like deciding whether to join a fraternity or sorority, commit to a party that might interfere with practice, or skip something important.

Scenario: A friend keeps pushing them to go to an event the night before a big game.

- **You:** "Okay, your friend keeps asking you to go out the night before your game. You want to say no, but you don't want to let them down. What can you do?"

- **Your Child:** "I could say I'll think about it and let them know later."

- **You:** "That's perfect. Give yourself time to think it through. If you're still not sure, just say, 'I'll pass.' You don't have to give in right away."

4. Normalize Making Mistakes

No matter how much we prepare them, our kids are going to make mistakes. It's part of growing up. The goal isn't perfection—it's giving them the confidence to make smart decisions most of the time, and to learn from their mistakes when they do mess up.

Let your child know that it's okay to make a mistake. What matters is how they handle it afterward. Encourage them to take responsibility, learn from the experience, and move forward. This helps reduce the fear of failure and empowers them to keep making thoughtful choices.

Key Action Steps for Parents:

- **Start the conversation early:** Don't wait until they're packing for college to talk about peer pressure and decision-making. Begin having these conversations in high school, so they have time to practice thinking through their choices.

- **Role-play real scenarios:** Practice casual ways to say no, think through consequences, and slow down when feeling pressured.

- **Teach the W.A.I.T. method:** Remind them that it's okay to pause and think before they act. Slowing down can prevent impulsive mistakes.

- **Encourage self-confidence:** Help them understand that confidence comes from within. They don't need to go along with the crowd to fit in.

- **Reinforce that mistakes are part of learning:** Let them know that it's okay to make a mistake—what matters is how they move forward from it.

Final Thoughts

Peer pressure is inevitable. Your student-athlete will face moments when they feel torn between what they know is right and what everyone else is doing. But by planting the seeds of good decision-making early, teaching them to think before they act, and giving them the tools to navigate tough situations, you'll be giving them the confidence to handle those moments wisely.

At the end of the day, it's about trusting the foundation you've laid and knowing that, even when they're faced with tough choices, they have the ability to make smart decisions—and learn from the ones they don't.

CHAPTER 7

USE YOUR VOICE, BECAUSE YOU CAN'T BORROW MINE

When Jordan passed away on June 13, 2018, I had two options: I could go down a rabbit hole of depression and emotional despair, or I could choose the second option—to turn our pain into purpose.

We decided to start the **Jordan McNair Foundation** on June 16, 2018, just three days after he passed away. Of course, like with any mission, what you start with evolves over time. But one thing has remained constant: our commitment to educating student-athletes about heat-related injuries and promoting awareness around how to stay safe on and off the field. I had a lot of time for self-reflection during those two weeks when Jordan was fighting for his life. I kept asking myself countless questions:

- *"What did I miss?"*

- *"What didn't I teach him when he was younger that could have helped protect him better?"*

- *"If I don't know these things how many other parents in America don't know them as well?*

And that's when I had a painful realization. As I mentioned earlier in this book, I had always taught Jordan to be coachable. Whatever the coach said was the right thing to do. I never taught him the **life-saving skill of self-advocacy**—how to speak up when something felt wrong, even when it meant questioning authority. I had taught him to respect adults, especially coaches, without ever showing him how to respectfully advocate for himself.

One of the core principles of the **Jordan McNair Foundation** is teaching student-athletes to listen to their bodies. Our motto is simple:

"When your body tells you to stop, stop."

"When you feel uncomfortable around a coach or adult, speak up."

But I didn't teach Jordan that when he was growing up. I was the average "athlete dad" who wanted to toughen him up, teaching him not to complain, to "rub some dirt on it" and keep going. I taught him to stand up for himself and not be afraid to fight among his peers, but I failed to teach him where the fine line is when it comes to self-advocacy and respect toward adults. I've beaten myself up for years over that. Looking back, I realized that I should have started planting seeds of self-advocacy when he first started playing sports as a little kid.

What parent thinks about going beyond the surface when they ask their child, "Is everything okay?" and get a one-word response? Most of us take those one-line answers at face value. I fell into that category too. But self-advocacy means teaching our kids that it's not only okay to speak up—it's necessary, especially when it comes to their health and well-being.

Why Self-Advocacy Matters

Self-advocacy is key to a student-athlete's success both on and off the field, especially at the collegiate level. Through my **KOBY Blueprint Unleashed Podcast**, where I interview collegiate student-athletes, I always ask one key question: **"What's one thing you wish you had learned in high school to help you transition into college?"**

The answer is almost always the same: **"I wish I had learned self-advocacy earlier—how to talk with professors and coaches."**

This is a recurring theme with so many student-athletes. They enter college without the skills to speak up for themselves in important situations, whether it's asking for help in a class, voicing concerns to a coach, or advocating for their mental and physical well-being. And that's where we, as parents, come in. The earlier we start **planting the seeds of self-advocacy**, the better prepared they'll be for every situation they encounter, from academics to athletics to social life.

Self-advocacy isn't just about teaching your child to "stand up" to people. It's about teaching them to communicate effectively, to know when to ask for help, and to trust that their voice matters, even when they're speaking to someone in a position of authority.

Key Lessons on Self-Advocacy

1. Being coachable doesn't mean being silent:
As parents, we want our kids to respect their coaches and teachers, but respect doesn't mean they should suffer in silence. Being coachable means listening, learning, and following directions but it also means speaking up when something feels off. Teach your child that advocating for their health, safety, and well-being isn't a sign of disrespect—it's a sign of strength.

2. Teach them how to respectfully express concerns:
Self-advocacy isn't about being defiant or confrontational—it's about communicating concerns in a calm and respectful way. Role-play situations with your child where they might need to speak up, such as:

○ Telling a coach they feel unwell during practice.

○ Asking a professor for clarification on an assignment or requesting extra help.

○ Voicing concerns about something happening on campus.

3. Help them practice **what to say** and **how to say it**, so they feel more confident when they're in real situations.

4. **Normalize asking for help:**
Many student-athletes fear that asking for help will make them look weak. Teach them that **asking for help is a form of strength**, not weakness. Whether it's reaching out to a counselor for mental health support, approaching a coach about feeling overworked, or seeking academic help, they need to know that it's okay to speak up when they're struggling.

5. **Start early:**
The earlier you start planting the seeds of self-advocacy, the better. It can begin with something as simple as encouraging your child to speak up when they don't understand something in class or need help with homework. Over time, those small moments build the confidence they'll need to advocate for themselves in higher-stakes situations.

Key Action Steps for Parents

1. **Role-play real-life scenarios:**
Sit down with your child and walk through different situations where they might need to advocate for themselves.

   ○ *"What would you say if you started feeling dizzy during practice?"*

   ○ *"How would you ask a professor for help if you were falling behind in a class?"*

   ○ *"How do I know when things aren't going well for me?*

   ○ *"What resources are on campus to support my mental health and well-being if I feel myself struggling?"*

2. **Teach them to ask questions:**
Encourage curiosity and critical thinking when making tough decisions. Whether it's questioning a coach's direction when they're unsure about something or asking for more information in class, remind them that it's okay to seek clarity.

3. **Model self-advocacy at home:**
Show them what it looks like to advocate for yourself. Whether it's at work, in a conversation with a service

provider, or in any real-world situation, model respectful self-advocacy so they can see it in action.

Final Thoughts

Teaching your student-athlete to be coachable is important —but teaching them to be vocal is critical. It could be the difference between staying silent when something feels wrong and speaking up when it matters most. Self-advocacy is a skill that will serve them for life, on and off the field.

As parents, we may not always be there to guide them through every experience, but if we plant the seeds of self-advocacy early, we can trust that they'll have the confidence to use their voice when they need it most.

CHAPTER 8

FINANCIAL LITERACY

"My First Credit Card Mistake"

I still remember my first credit card. I was in college, walking through the student union, when I saw a table set up with free pens, water bottles, and keychains. A man behind the table was calling students over, smiling and telling us, **"Sign up and get approved for your first credit card today!"**

I was nineteen. I didn't know anything about credit. I had been working since I was fifteen, but my mom and I never had a conversation about financial literacy or how credit worked. Like most broke college students, I thought, **"I can buy food now and pay for it later."**

So, I signed up.

That first credit card had a $500 limit. It felt like "free money" at the time. But that $500 cost me **almost double** in interest by the time I paid it off. I didn't understand the importance of paying on time, managing balances, or how interest worked. I learned the hard way.

And I wasn't the only one.

Back then, college students were constantly targeted by credit card companies. They'd set up tables at student unions, football games, and college fairs. They knew that eighteen- and nineteen-year-olds didn't know any better. It was a business strategy, and it worked.

It's different now.

Today, student-athletes aren't just signing up for $500 credit cards. They're signing NIL deals worth tens of thousands —sometimes hundreds of thousands—of dollars. Your child can literally earn more money in one semester than some of us make in a year.

That sounds great, right? Well, it is—but only if they know how to handle it.

If a nineteen-year-old me could blow through $500 on a credit card, imagine what a nineteen-year-old with $100,000 from an NIL deal might do. Without guidance, that money will disappear just as fast as it came in. And that's why I'm telling you this:

"A kid with a lot of money spells disaster if we don't properly teach them financial literacy."

Show Me the Money$

The NIL era is an opportunity, but it's also a **financial trap**.

For the first time in history, student-athletes can be paid for their name, image, and likeness. They can make money off sponsorships, endorsements, and brand deals. But there's one thing most people forget: **Money doesn't come with instructions.**

Here's what's happening right now:

- Young athletes are signing NIL deals and receiving huge payments.

- They're being offered sponsorships from sneaker companies, fast-food chains, and big-name brands.

- They're suddenly making more money than their parents—but they have no idea what to do with it.

This is why **financial literacy is crucial**. If we don't teach student-athletes how to manage this money, it will be gone as quickly as it came.

> **"It's not about how much money you make. It's about how much money you keep."**

And that's where financial literacy comes in.

Key Lessons for Parents

1. **Teach Them That $100 is NOT $100**

   ○ I have a nephew who plays football for a Big Ten school. I told him, **"Nephew, always remember that $100 is not $100."**

   ○ He looked at me, confused. I explained that taxes, fees, and other expenses mean that $100 will never be a full $100 in his pocket.

   ○ Teach your child how taxes work on NIL deals and why "$100,000" isn't really $100,000 after taxes, agents, and fees are taken out.

2. **Teach Them About Compound Interest**

   ○ Most elite athletes have never had a real job. Their "job" has been sports.

   ○ Teach them about **the power of compound interest**.

   ○ Show them how $100 invested at eighteen can turn into thousands by thirty if they save it.

3. **Teach Them the "Dr. J Rule"**

- When Charles Barkley was a young player in the NBA, **Julius Erving, a.k.a. Dr. J, gave him timeless advice**.

- Dr. J asked Charles how many cars he had. He said six. Dr. J asked how many houses he had. He said two.

- Dr. J said, **"Why? You can only drive one car at a time and live in one house at a time."**

- Teach your child to think like Dr. J—not like twenty-year-old Charles Barkley.

The Jordan McNair Safe and Fair Play Act

The NIL movement is about giving student-athletes the right to profit from their name, image, and likeness. But here's the truth: **How can you pay an athlete if you can't keep them safe?**

That was the heart of the Jordan McNair Safe and Fair Play Act, a bill we helped pass in the state of Maryland.

One of the most important provisions in this bill is a safety clause. It says that a university cannot threaten or revoke a student-athlete's scholarship because they're injured. It also says that a school **cannot rush an athlete back to play after an injury**.

This provision matters. Why? Because if you have a child earning money from NIL, but they're being rushed back from injury, what good is that money?

Money without safety is meaningless.

Maryland became the first state to pass this law with bipartisan support. It set a standard for other states to follow, and it represents the values of **fairness, safety, and protection for student-athletes.**

Action Steps for Parents

Here's how you can prepare your child for the financial realities of NIL money:

1. **Teach Them About Taxes**

   o   NIL money is taxed like regular income. Teach them that **$100,000 isn't $100,000.**

   o   Introduce them to basic tax forms (W-2, 1099) and talk to them about working with an accountant.

2. **Explain the Value of Investing**

   o   Teach them about compound interest and why early investing matters.

- Show them how to start a savings account, a Roth IRA, or an investment portfolio.

3. **Explain the "Dr. J Rule"**

- One car. One house. That's it.

- If Charles Barkley could learn this lesson, so can your child.

4. **Talk About the Financial Power of Attorney**

- If your child is signing NIL deals, they need financial support.

- A **power of attorney** can help them avoid bad deals or bad spending habits.

Reflection Questions for Parents and Student-Athletes

1. **If you signed an NIL deal today, what would you do with the money?**

2. **Do you know how much money you'd actually get after taxes, fees, and agent costs?**

3. **Do you know how to protect yourself from bad financial advice?**

Key Takeaways

1. "A kid with a lot of money spells disaster if they don't have financial literacy."

2. "$100 is never $100 after taxes and fees."

3. "How can you pay an athlete if you can't keep them safe?"

4. "Teach them to think like Dr. J, not twenty-year-old Charles Barkley."

CHAPTER 9

THE POWER OF NIL AND THE COLLECTIVE: WHAT YOU NEED TO KNOW

The NIL era has changed the game for student-athletes. For the first time in history, student-athletes can legally profit from their personal brand while in college—something that was unheard of just a few years ago. It's an exciting time, but it's also a complicated one. With money now on the table, there are new opportunities ... and new risks.

As a parent, your role isn't just to support your child in making the right athletic or academic decisions—it's also to **prepare them to make smart financial decisions**. The truth is, while NIL income can provide student-athletes with incredible financial freedom, without proper guidance, it can just as easily lead to financial trouble.

I spoke with a trusted sports agent and lawyer to help answer some of the most important questions parents should ask about NIL and collective deals and how to navigate this new landscape. Below are **ten key questions and answers** that every parent and student-athlete should understand before jumping into an NIL contract.

Ten Questions for a Sports Agent Regarding NIL Contracts, Collective Deals, and Financial Literacy

1. What are the most important things parents and student-athletes should understand before signing an NIL deal?

First, whether the deal is for traditional marketing outside of the university (e.g., retail) or whether it is a deal with the collective/university determines what's important.

If the deal is **traditional marketing**, the key is understanding:

- **What are the deliverables?** What exactly does the athlete need to do?

- **Are there conflicts?** Does the deal conflict with the school's existing marketing partners?

- If the deal is with the **collective/university**, focus on:

- **Payment amount and schedule**—How much are they being paid, and when?

- **Termination terms**—Can the deal be terminated at any time, and under what conditions?

I strongly advise all parents and student-athletes to have an experienced agent or lawyer review every NIL deal before signing.

2. Are there any red flags to watch for in NIL contracts that might indicate a bad or exploitative deal?

One major red flag I've seen is **termination for convenience** clauses. This allows a collective to terminate the contract with very short notice (e.g., ten days) for no specific reason.

This means that in the middle of the season, a collective could decide to stop paying the student-athlete, leaving them without any recourse. Avoid any deal with termination terms like this.

3. How can parents help their student-athletes protect themselves legally when negotiating or signing NIL deals?

The easiest and most effective way to protect a student-athlete is to have an **experienced agent or lawyer** review every contract before signing.

NIL deals involve legal language and terms that most people—especially young people—won't fully understand. A professional can help ensure there are no hidden clauses or terms that could harm the athlete.

4. Would you recommend hiring a lawyer or agent to review NIL contracts? If so, what should families look for when selecting someone to represent their child?

Absolutely, 100 percent. Look for someone with:

- **Experience negotiating professional contracts** with professional clubs or organizations, ideally specific to your sport.

- **Experience in high-level marketing deals** with major corporations.

- Be wary of "street agents"—individuals who may not have the proper credentials or experience to handle these kinds of contracts.

5. What are the most common financial mistakes student-athletes make when they start earning NIL income, and how can they avoid them?

The most common mistake is **not saving money for taxes**.

NIL deals are typically structured as **1099 income**, meaning student-athletes are treated as independent contractors. Unlike a regular paycheck, where taxes are automatically withheld, student-athletes are responsible for paying their taxes.

Many student-athletes don't realize that **20-35 percent of their NIL income will go to taxes**, and they often don't set aside enough money to cover that burden. I recommend working with an accountant to properly handle taxes and finances.

6. How should student-athletes manage taxes on NIL income, and what steps can parents take to help them stay compliant with the IRS?

Before the student-athlete receives any payment, parents should work with their agent or lawyer to vet a **tax professional**.

Setting up the right structure—such as receiving payments through a company instead of as an individual—can help with tax compliance and overall financial management.

7. Do you have any tips for student-athletes on balancing short-term spending with long-term saving or investing?

My advice is simple:

- **If they have enough to invest, they should.** Their future self will thank them.

- NIL income gives many student-athletes a head start on building financial stability, even if they don't go pro.

- That said, they should still enjoy a portion of their earnings. This money is a reward for their hard work, and it's okay to spend some of it—but within reason and according to a budget.

8. How can student-athletes use NIL income to build financial stability, even if they don't go on to play professionally?

The key is becoming **financially literate**—understanding how to budget, save, and invest.

Surround the student-athlete with a **team of advisers** who care about their long-term success, not just their athletic performance. By learning how to make their money work for them now, they'll set themselves up for financial freedom later.

9. What's one piece of financial advice you give to young athletes to help them stay grounded and avoid financial pitfalls?

Understand that **this is just the beginning**. No matter how much money you make through NIL, you still have a long life to live. Use this platform to create a solid financial foundation for the future.

Also, learn how to say **NO**. No to friends, no to family—protect yourself first, so you can be in a better position to help others later.

10. What's the biggest misconception parents and student-athletes have about NIL deals, and how can they better prepare for the realities of the NIL landscape?

The biggest misconception is that most NIL deals are for **traditional marketing**—things like commercials, sponsorships, and endorsements from major companies. The reality is that only a handful of student-athletes get those kinds of deals.

The majority of NIL deals right now are through **collectives**, which means that athletes are being paid by **groups affiliated with the schools that pool funds from donors, alumni, and sponsors to compensate student-athletes for their name, image, and likeness**. Focus on being great at your sport and building your social media presence to attract real marketing opportunities.

Final Thoughts

The NIL era is a game changer, but it also comes with new responsibilities. Your child's ability to make smart financial decisions now can set them up for long-term success—even if they don't go pro. Surround them with a strong team, help them become financially literate, and remind them to think beyond the game.

As parents, your job is to help them navigate this exciting yet complex world of NIL so that the money **works for them, not the other way around**.

CHAPTER 10:

EMPOWERING YOUR STUDENT-ATHLETE FOR LIFE

The purpose of this book is simple: to **educate, prepare**, and **equip your student-athlete** for the next chapter of their life, both in sports and beyond. Whether they go on to play at the collegiate level or transition into life outside of athletics, my goal is to provide you with the tools to guide them through this journey.

The **5th Quarter** offers insight and practical strategies for teaching your child how to:

- **Advocate for themselves,**

- **Protect themselves** physically, mentally, and financially,

- And make smart decisions not every time, but hopefully most of the time.

It's always the little things we tend to overlook until we're forced to deal with them. By reading this book, I hope you'll be able to **prepare your child ahead of time**, so they don't have to learn all those lessons the hard way.

Your Voice, Their Voice

Remember this: **The older they get, the smaller our voice becomes.**

At the youth level, your voice is loud. You're on the sidelines, calling plays, giving advice, and cheering them on. But then they enter high school, and you start to notice something—the coaches begin to take control, and you're not as involved anymore. By the time they reach college, you'll barely have a seat at the table. In fact, the only time you might share the same air with a college coach could be during the recruitment process or an official visit.

This is why teaching your child to **advocate for themselves** is critical to their success. You won't always be there to speak for them, so they have to learn how to speak up for themselves.

Please, give them that voice of **self-advocacy**.

I wish there had been a book like this for me to read when Jordan was going through the recruitment process. It might have made a difference. As a father, I taught him to be coachable. To me, that meant doing whatever the coach said without question, trusting that the coach always knew best. But looking back, I realize that wasn't enough.

I never taught him to speak up if he ever felt uncomfortable around a coach or saw something concerning happen to a teammate. I never taught him that being coachable didn't mean being silent when something didn't feel right. That was my mistake, and it's something I'll always carry with me.

Life After the Game

Empower your student-athlete not just for **their time on the field**, but for **life after the ball stops bouncing** and the game of sports is over. Because one day, the game will end— but life keeps going. And when it does, they'll need the confidence, skills, and voice to navigate the world on their own.

This is about more than sports. It's about preparing them for **the game of life**.

A Call to Action

As parents, we may not be able to prevent every tough situation our kids will face. We can't always be there to protect them from bad decisions, difficult moments, or challenging environments. But what we can do is **give them the tools they need to protect themselves**. Teach them to speak up. Teach them to think critically. Teach them to prioritize their safety and well-being—and remind them that they are never alone, no matter how far away they may be.

Start planting those seeds of self-advocacy, financial literacy, and mental well-being now. They may not listen to everything today, but one day those lessons will take root, and they'll be grateful you took the time to prepare them.

A Legacy of Preparedness

Looking back, I realize that the biggest lessons are often the smallest things, the things we tend to miss until it's too late. My hope is that this book helps you catch those moments. That it helps you prepare your student-athlete not just for success in sports, but for life itself.

This isn't just Jordan's story. It's a blueprint for every parent who wants to see their child thrive not just while they're on the field, but long after the final whistle blows.

Final Words

Take Action to Prepare Your Student-Athlete

There's no way to predict every challenge your child will face, but there is a way to prepare them. By teaching them to advocate for themselves, think critically, and make smart decisions, you're giving them something far more valuable than athletic success: you're giving them the tools they'll need to thrive in the game of life.

This isn't just about preparing for sports; it's about preparing for life. Start planting those seeds today. They may not listen to everything right away, but one day, those lessons will take root, and they'll be grateful you took the time to guide them.

"Prepare them for the game of life, so when the final whistle blows, they'll be ready for whatever comes next."

First-Generation Student-Athletes: Preparation Beyond Recruitment

For many student-athletes, going to college is a family milestone. They're often the **first person in their family to attend college**—a proud and momentous achievement that carries the hopes and dreams of an entire family.

I've seen far too many stories of **first-generation** student-athletes from inner-city urban backgrounds getting scholarships to play at colleges across the nation. Their families are thrilled to see them break generational barriers, leave their neighborhoods, and pursue their dreams.

Take, for example, a family I spoke with recently. Their son, James, had been the **first in their family** to attend college on a basketball scholarship. He was their pride and joy, a beacon of hope for his younger siblings. But within a few months of starting school, James started coming home every chance he got. He wanted to stay connected to his childhood friends, who were not always the best influences. Over time, his grades slipped, and his focus on basketball waned. He eventually left school and returned home—a heartbreaking example of how quickly a once-promising opportunity can slip away.

This experience is not unique. According to the NCAA, **about one in five student-athletes (20 percent) identifies as a first-generation college student**, with the numbers varying depending on the division:

- **Division I**: Approximately 17 percent of student-athletes are **first-generation** college students.

- **Division II**: This number increases to around 27 percent.

- **Division III**: Roughly 18 percent of student-athletes identify as **first-generation**.

Graduation rates for **first-generation** student-athletes are not comprehensively documented across all divisions and sports. However, current data provides some promising insights:

- **Division II**: Student-athletes in Division II generally have **higher graduation rates** compared to the overall student body. With a significant proportion of **first-**

generation students in this division, these athletes are accessing and succeeding in higher education at commendable rates.

- **Overall Trends**: The NCAA reports that student-athletes often graduate at rates equal to or higher than their nonathlete peers. For instance, the **graduation success rate (GSR)** for Division I student-athletes has risen from **74 percent in 2002 to 91 percent in 2024**, reflecting long-term improvements in academic outcomes.

(*Disclaimer: These are not all the statistics available, but they reflect current trends and progress in academic achievement for student-athletes.*)

The numbers show that a significant portion of student-athletes are not only navigating the challenges of college sports, but they are also breaking generational barriers in their families by attending college for the first time. This is a major achievement, but it also comes with additional pressures and obstacles that aren't always discussed.

There are many reasons things may not work out for **first-generation** student-athletes at the collegiate level:

- **Culture shock**: Adjusting to life in a new environment—especially one far from home or where few people share their background—can be overwhelming.

- **Mental health challenges**: Balancing academics, athletics, and the social pressures of college life often leads to anxiety, depression, or burnout.

- **Unpreparedness**: Some students may struggle to manage the demands of college because they were never taught essential life skills like time management, self-advocacy, or how to handle adversity.

- **Unrealistic expectations for success**: Many student-athletes and their families pin everything on dreams of going pro, only to find the odds aren't in their favor. Without a clear plan for life beyond sports, they can feel lost or defeated when things don't go as planned.

This is why **the goal isn't just to get to the next level—it's to stay there and thrive.**

Whenever I speak to college athletes, I emphasize this:

"Your friends back home would love to trade places with you. Don't squander this opportunity. Take advantage of your education, resources, and support."

As parents, your role doesn't end once your child steps onto a college campus. It's just the beginning of a new chapter where your support, guidance, and preparation are more critical than ever. Talk to your student-athlete about the challenges they may face—from culture shock and mental health struggles to managing time and adjusting expectations. Encourage them to stay focused on the bigger picture and to fully embrace the opportunities in front of them.

Sports is a tool—a gateway to many things in life. And while success in athletics is always celebrated, one of the most valuable things sports can lead to is a **good education.** Education is the foundation that will give your child better opportunities long after the final whistle blows.

The path may not always be easy, but the lessons you teach now will shape the way your child handles adversity and builds their future. Help them see that success isn't defined solely by points scored or games won. The real victory is earning an education, developing as a person, and preparing for life after the game ends.

By keeping them grounded, holding them accountable, and reminding them of their long-term goals, you can help them make the most of this once-in-a-lifetime opportunity. Remember: **It's not just about making it to the next level— it's about staying there and thriving.**

AUTHOR'S NOTE: A FATHER'S WISH

I remember something my uncle once told me when Jordan was a teenager. He said, **"Marty, you have both of his ears right now. Always try to keep at least one of them, because you'll most definitely lose the other to all the outside influences Jordan will meet along the way in his journey."**

That advice stuck with me.

When they're young, you have their full attention. You're their **coach**, their **protector**, their **cheerleader**—the voice they trust most. But as they grow, you start to compete with the outside world for that influence. Coaches, teammates, friends, social media, and recruiters all begin to fill their world with new voices, and no matter how hard you try, you realize that **you won't always have both of their ears**.

I wrote this book because I understand how easy it is to assume you've done enough to prepare your child, only to realize later that **what you don't know can hurt them**. I thought I had covered all the bases with Jordan. I taught him to be respectful, coachable, and tough. I believed I had prepared him for everything life would throw at him on and off the field.

But what I didn't know—and what I didn't teach him—became fatal. That's a pain no parent should ever have to live with.

This book isn't just about **recruitment, scholarships**, or **NIL deals**. It's about something far more important: preparing your child for the world beyond sports. It's about **asking tough questions, teaching them to advocate for themselves**, and **ensuring they're ready for life when the ball stops bouncing**.

For more insight on **student-athlete self-advocacy and preparation**, I encourage you to partner with the **Jordan McNair Foundation** through our **KOBY (Keep On Believing In Yourself) College Readiness Curriculum**. This program is designed to equip student-athletes with the tools they need to succeed both **on and off the field**, and to prepare them for life's challenges beyond sports. Visit www.kobyblueprint.com to learn more about how we're helping young athletes develop life skills, leadership, and self-advocacy.

Additionally, subscribe to the **Jordan McNair Foundation YouTube Channel** to watch **The KOBY Blueprint Unleashed Podcast**, where collegiate student-athletes share their real-life stories of balancing **academics, athletics**, and **personal life**. For more information about our mission, ongoing work, and resources, visit The Jordan McNair Foundation website.

If you're looking for a deeper dive into the **questions parents should ask during the recruitment process**, I encourage you to check out my first book, *Can My Child Play?*

The Questions We Should Have Asked. That book tells Jordan's story and provides a guide to help parents navigate the **critical decisions** they'll face as they support their student-athletes and advocate for their safety in sports.

If you'd like to **book me, Marty McNair, to speak to your team or organization**, please contact me via **contact@thejordanmcnairfoundation.org** or visit **thejordanmcnairfoundation.org**. Whether it's about the recruitment process, injury prevention, mental health, or building life skills for student-athletes, I would be honored to share my story and offer guidance to help empower young athletes and their families.

Finally, my uncle's advice reminds me of something else: even if you only keep **one ear**, that's enough to make a difference. So, keep talking. Keep guiding. Keep preparing them for the life ahead, even when it feels like they're not listening. Because one day, those lessons will take root, and they'll remember everything you taught them.

Thank you for trusting me to be part of your journey. I wish you and your student-athlete a lifetime of **health**, **success** and, most importantly, **purpose**—long after the game ends.

With heartfelt gratitude,

Marty McNair

ACKNOWLEDGMENT

If you had told me eight years ago that this would become my life's journey, I wouldn't have believed you. Back then, I was just a father like any other—someone who wanted nothing more than to see his child succeed. Like every parent, there was nothing I wouldn't do, within reason and law, to support Jordan's dreams and help him achieve his athletic success on the field and in life. But in my case, what started as a mission to ensure his future has transformed into something greater: ensuring that his **legacy** saves the lives of others.

I want to express my deepest gratitude to every **family member**, **friend**, **supporter**, **colleague**, and **partner** who has stood by our side and supported the work of the **Jordan McNair Foundation**. Whether through your time, your contributions, or simply your words of encouragement, you've played a crucial role in helping us pursue our mission to promote awareness, education, and safety for student-athletes. Over the past six years, your support has made a real difference, and for that, I am forever grateful.

A **special thanks** to **Attorney Aston Wilson**, who offered clear and valuable insight into the **NIL landscape** and how to best protect and prepare your student-athlete's potential financial opportunities. His expertise helped ensure that this guide provides real, actionable information for parents navigating the complexities of NIL deals. He can be reached at **Aston@astonlaw.com**.

Jordan's legacy lives on through the lives we've touched and the change we continue to fight for. None of this would have been possible without you—thank you for believing in our mission and standing with us. Together, we will continue to honor Jordan by ensuring that no other parent has to endure what we went through.

ABOUT THE AUTHOR

Marty McNair is a father, advocate, speaker, and author who has dedicated his life to raising awareness about student-athlete safety and equipping families with the tools they need to protect and prepare their children for life on and off the field.

Marty's journey into advocacy began after the tragic passing of his son, **Jordan McNair**, from a heat-related injury during a college football practice in 2018. Determined to turn his personal pain into purpose, Marty co-founded the **Jordan McNair Foundation**, which focuses on promoting awareness, education, and prevention of heat-related injuries in sports. The foundation has since become a nationally recognized organization, helping to improve safety protocols for student-athletes across the country.

In addition to his work with the foundation, Marty has authored two books:

- ***Can My Child Play?*** *The Questions We Should Have Asked,* which highlights the critical questions parents should ask to protect their student-athletes during the recruitment process.

- ***The 5th Quarter:*** *"A Parent's Guide to Preparing Student Athletes For Life Beyond the Game,"* is a comprehensive guide designed to help parents and student-athletes navigate the complex realities of collegiate sports, from recruitment and NIL deals to mental health and self-advocacy.

Marty is a sought-after speaker who has shared his story and insights with schools, athletic programs, and organizations nationwide. His mission is to not only honor Jordan's legacy but to ensure that no other family has to endure a preventable loss. Through his work, he empowers parents to advocate for their children and student-athletes to advocate for themselves.

When he's not speaking or working on foundation initiatives, Marty enjoys spending time with his family, mentoring young athletes, and continuing to develop programs that support student-athlete readiness and safety.

Connect with Marty McNair

- **Email:** contact@thejordanmcnairfoundation.org

- **Website:** thejordanmcnairfoundation.org

- **Social Media:** IG thejordanmcnairfoundation, Linkedin @Martin Marty McNair